Sacred Listening

From Fear to Love

MARGARET J. COAN

BALBOA.PRESS

A DIVISION OF HAY HOUSE

Balboa Press books may be ordered through booksellers or by contacting:

Balboa Press
A Division of Hay House
1663 Liberty Drive
Bloomington, IN 47403
www.balboapress.com
1 (877) 407-4847

Print information available on the last page.

ISBN: 978-1-4525-5363-4 (sc)
ISBN: 978-1-4525-5362-7 (e)

Library of Congress Control Number: 2012910827

Balboa Press rev. date: 04/03/2020

Sacred Listening

God guide me
Teach me
Show me

How to listen with my heart

How to hear the questions
behind the answers

How to hear the hurt
behind the anger

How to hear the need
behind the accomplishment

How to hear the fear
behind the arrogance

How to hear the hope
behind the despair

How to hear Your Truth
behind every moment

How to always hear Your Love...

Written in Loving Devotion To:

Jesus & Mary *who guide and lead me in each moment*
toward our true home of love without conditions.

Dedicated in love to:

My husband John and our Sacred Trinity
Michael
The music of my heart.
Patrick
The silence of my soul.
Ryan
The dance of my spirit.

Special Acknowledgement for:

Grace Metz *whose loving listening opened my heart into blossom and encouraged me to write this book.*

To every member of my family, friends and neighbors who have taught me about love.

To all of nature in its infinite beauty that connects me to my soul.

To life itself for each Sacred moment.

Contents

Introduction

My purpose in writing this book is to stop hiding, to heal in the speaking of my experience and to connect to others who have similar challenges, questions and struggles.

I write because writing is my life raft, the way I stay afloat when the storms of life want to pull me under. Writing is a form of prayer for me, a source of deep connection to my higher power (God). Often when I write the experience is that of someone else writing through me and I am simply the recording instrument. I feel I have been invited to share my experience with how the Holy One has transformed my inner life from one grounded in fear to one grounded in love.

The process of creating this book has taken me on a wonderful journey of healing. I experienced each chapter as it was being written through me. I learned so much about myself and my relationship to trust, being open, silence, feelings, healing and wisdom. I experienced the tremendous difference between knowing something in my mind and living it through my heart to every cell of my being.

This process of having an idea and bringing it into physical form has been like giving birth to all my fears. I have to constantly surrender to my higher self and ask for courage, strength and guidance. My faith in a loving divine creator grew tremendously through this process. I became aware that courage, strength, endurance, and perseverance live in my spiritual core where infinite possibilities exist. I know that the more I trust in God, myself and others, the more wondrous is my day-to-day living.

My intention, prayer and hope for this book is that each reader has a similar experience of new understanding of themselves, God and others in their life. I pray that the transformation that occurs in each life ripples loving healing and reconciliation to all it touches.

I hope that as we each learn to listen more deeply and compassionately to ourselves that we will come to unity of understanding. I pray that we each will be willing to let go of our prejudices, certainties, self-reliance, and self-centeredness so we can open our hearts and minds to the infinite possibilities born in faith.

Peace Joy Love Be Always With You

Suggestions How to Use This Book

Through the process of turning my dream of writing a book into a concrete reality, I learned the absolute necessity of discipline, order and structure. Each day I incorporated writing in my daily schedule knowing it was as important to the healing of my soul as prayer and meditation. My intention, commitment and schedule were all important practices in my learning to honor and love myself.

I encourage each of you to commit to spending time each day to read, reflect and actively participate in the exercises offered. Think of this time as a sacred gift of loving yourself as you connect more intimately with the Divine Being (God), with yourself and with your brothers and sister. This daily practice may challenge you in many ways and I encourage you to meet each challenge as an opportunity to connect to your true self that longs to be free.

As you embark on this inner journey, creating a special place to go each day is very helpful. This should be a space that is removed from the noise and busyness of your life. Set this area up with items that open your spirit in love such as pictures, candles, stones, gems etc.

Now that you have made a commitment and set up a place to go each day, it is time to open the book. You will notice that the structure of this book is designed to engage the reader in active participation. Each chapter begins with a short reflection that is followed by six days of journal prompts, experiential exercises, and holy listening; the 7th day is a weekly review. You will get the most from the book if you follow the order it has been written, completing each chapter before going to the next.

I applaud your courage in deciding to embark on your spiritual awakening. I encourage you to continue if it gets hard. This is an opportunity to learn to listen to parts of yourself that have been in hiding and are waiting for you to welcome them back home in your heart. As you connect to your true inner spirit, you will be graced into freedom, healing, and wholeness.

My heart and prayers are with each of you as you embark on your soul's awakening. It is a wondrous journey uniquely designed for each one of us. Your life will be transformed from living in fear to living in love.

Peace Joy Love Be Always With You

CHAPTER I

TRUST

Introduction

Have you ever thought about how trees are planted deeply in the earth that nourishes their entire being? How they are centered in still calmness at their roots and naturally surrender their life to each season?

As my mind soaked in these wonderings, it occurred to me that the strength of the deeply grounded roots enable the branches to be flexible to sway and move with the wind and let go of the attire of each season that opens to the next. Indeed, the tree transforms its outer form from lush shading green to reds, yellows, crispy browns, to naked emptiness and birthing buds and blossoms. While the tree gracefully robes and disrobes its outer garments, the roots remain strongly planted in the earthy soil.

Could it be that for each of us, trust is like the earthy soil for the tree? Is it possible that trust is the essential and necessary element for living life in all its various expressions and forms? Are we able to be fully alive, authentic and free if we are not deeply grounded in the soil of trust?

As I continued to contemplate these questions, it occurred to me that where we plant our trust will determine the fruit of the tree. Can we be healthy if we are deeply rooted in the soil of people, places and things that live outside of our self? Can we ever fill the empty longings that live within each of us in the soil of success, accomplishments, riches, power, or control? Could it be that trying to plant ourselves in the outer manifestations of the world only serves to deplete our soil from its nutrients that already live within our being? Is it possible the spiritual journey is the soil to plant our trust? Could it be as we seek the truth we discover true love and freedom are born as we let go into full surrender? Is it possible that opening to our spiritual reality connects us to the only soil that can plant us deeply and allow our limbs to bend and sway in the experience of each moment?

Would you like to be open, free, clinging to nothing, trusting that each season of your living invites you to bend and sway with the wind? Would you like to plant your tree in soil that is always rich in wisdom, understanding and compassion?

This chapter invites you to open your heart and mind to discover where your trust is grounded. The exercises are designed to connect you to the spiritual soil, which contains all the nutrients to become the unique wondrous tree you were created to be.

Personal Reflection

As I gaze backwards on my living I notice that I was living in a beautiful forest filled with oaks, weeping willows, birches, and pines. I spent many joyous hours with each one wishing I could be them; wanting to be every tree but the one I was designed to be. I tried to find my nourishing soil and plant my roots in all the trees I met. I would change my outer appearance from moment to moment hoping to find one that could fill my empty longings for deep roots, rich soil and flowing limbs. I kept trying to get my oxygen in the other's soil not understanding I needed to plant roots of my own.

I had to learn to stop hiding from myself, stop running from the truth and stand still long enough to discover the tree I was created to be. It was time to be silent and listen to the life living inside me. I yearned to awaken the calm still center of my being.

I yearned to be deeply rooted so I could endure each season of my living strong and sure in my center. I longed to be whole, flowing and flexible in each precious moment.

Experience has taught me the only soil that can nourish these longings and yearnings is the divine creator that lives and breathes and has its being in my center, your center, our center. I understand all my suffering has been a result of being attached to people, places and things that do not have the power to nurture and complete me. I have come to believe that God puts these longings in our heart to bring us each back home to our true selves; spiritual beings created in love to love.

With my roots centered in the rich soil of trust, my heart has been opened to the beautiful fruits of each season. Indeed, I have discovered the tree that I am; a weeping willow perched on the edge of the sea; longing, waiting, and trusting all is in the order it is meant to be.

"Trust is a rich word laden with meaning and direction for your life."
(Sarah Young)

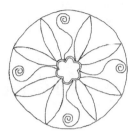

Day 1
Journal Prompts...

🌀 Observe the rhythm of your life. Where are your roots planted?

🌀 What brings meaning and direction in your life?

🌀 Are you living the life that wants to live in you?

"Trust is a rich word laden with meaning and direction for your life."
(Sarah Young)

Experiential Exercise

(Walking Meditation – bring your journal)

Go to a favorite place outside that nourishes your spirit, ideally away from your day-to-day cares and concerns. Observe the beauty around you, breathe it in and be nourished. Notice the sky, the birds, the trees, the fauna, the air, the sun, and the wind. Become present to the gift that each of these beings brings to your spirit. Walk for a few minutes to get present to your outer world and your inner world.

Once you feel fully present, ponder the question what do I trust in? Stepping in rhythm with your gate keep repeating this questions (silently or aloud if you prefer) I trust in _____?

Allow your thoughts to flow freely while continuing to come back to this question. Try not to change or edit what arises, just simply notice.

When you finish your walk jot down what the experience was like. Write down anything that you learned about trust or a list of things that you trust in. What have you learned about yourself and trust?

"Trust is a rich word laden with meaning and direction for your life."
(Sarah Young)

Holy Listening

(Read 3 times silently and/or out loud. Notice word or words that seem to be calling for your attention. Sit in silence listening to their message. Write a reflection.)

Wait in Trust

Do not
run
away
Do not
fight
against

WAIT IN TRUST

Experience
each moment
fully
Open to
its
language

LIVE IN FAITH

Where fear
unfolds into
unconditional
Love

AND ALL THINGS ARE POSSIBLE

*"Follow your heart but be quiet for awhile first – ask questions than
feel the wisdom – learn to trust your heart."*
(unknown author)

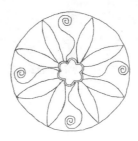

Day 2
Journal Prompts...

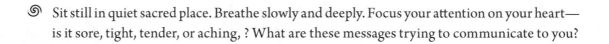

🌀   Sit still in quiet sacred place. Breathe slowly and deeply. Focus your attention on your heart—is it sore, tight, tender, or aching, ? What are these messages trying to communicate to you?

🌀   If you knew you only had three more days on earth what would you do? Whom would you be with? What would you share that is on your heart?

🌀   Allow yourself to dream without considering being "realistic". What do you long for in your life? What would an ideal life look like for you?

"Follow your heart but be quiet for awhile first – ask questions than feel the wisdom – learn to trust your heart."
(unknown author)

Experiential Exercise

(Guided Journey with Spiritual Guide)

Sit quietly in sacred space and breathe slowly and deeply. Let go of all your concerns and things to do. Relax and allow yourself to be fully present to this guided experience.

Guided journey:

Allow your imagination to bring you to a favorite place (could be the ocean, river, mountains, church, temple, or by the fire,…). Once you have arrived at your favorite place, observe your surroundings in detail; notice the smells, tastes, textures, sights, and sounds. Soak in the presence of serenity and peace. Invite a spiritual guide/teacher to join you (can be anyone of your choice). Sit across from one another in silence soaking in the gift of being together. Ask this loving guide to be a space of listening to everything that is in your heart; ; your joys, your sorrows, your fears, your questions, your hopes, and your dreams. Do not edit anything. Allow all your feelings and emotions a place to be fully received. Share all with this loving guide. When you have emptied your heart, go back into silence sitting across from your guide. Stay still and silent allowing yourself to absorb all healing grace the guide has for you. Wait for your guide to share with you their wisdom and guidance. TRUST in your listening.

Write a reflection in your journal.

"Follow your heart but be quiet for awhile first – ask questions than feel the wisdom – learn to trust your heart."
(unknown author)

Holy Listening

(Read 3 times silently and/or out loud. Notice word or words that seem to be calling for your attention. Sit in silence listening to their message. Write a reflection.)

"… we must learn to trust our own inner wisdom. For years, I denied my intuition, my gut feelings, and my mental acuity. It was terrible, painful deprivation that I have worked to overcome. We all need to trust our own minds, our own feelings, our own emotions, our senses and our bodies. When we do so there is a wonderful blending of the inner and the outer. We can become receptive to our partners (all our relationships) and the lessons they have for us.

Some people find themselves continually rejecting the lessons their partners and the people close to them offer. They feel that others are letting them down. Sometimes our loved ones do fail us, but just as often, the gap may actually be caused by our own lack of self-trust. If we keep saying 'I trust these people and they keep disappointing me,' then it may be that we are actually disappointing ourselves. If we are out of harmony with ourselves, not listening to our own inner whisperings about what is safe and true, the proper message cannot get through. And we feel let down." *(Patricia Love)*

"Trust is the fruit of a relationship which you know you are loved."
(Author Unknown)

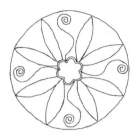

Day 3
Journal Prompts...

🌀 Who do you trust? Are you confident of their love for you?

🌀 Can love exist without trust?

🌀 What comes first, trust or love? Could it be they only exist together?

"Trust is the fruit of a relationship which you know you are loved."
(Author Unknown)

Experiential Exercise

(Letter to God about trust)

Begin by a breath prayer: Breathing in: I trust you…
Breathing out… with my life.

Once you feel present, centered and calm, begin a letter to God asking him about trust and how he is enough for you. Ask him to show you what is holding you back from complete trust in his divine goodness and love. Ask him to show you where you need to grow in trust. Ask him to give you wisdom and understanding about trust. Does giving trust help another become trustworthy? Is it unwise to trust everyone? How can I discern who to trust? Is trust based on another's behavior or my faith in God's power to transform?

"Trust is the fruit of a relationship which you know you are loved."
(Author Unknown)

Holy Listening

(Read 3 times slowly. Notice the word or words calling for your attention. Sit in silence allowing them to speak to you. Write a reflection.)

Let nothing disturb thee
Nothing affright thee
All things are passing
God never changes
Patient endurance attained to all things
Who God possess in nothing is wanting
Alone God suffices
(St. Teresa of Avila)

"We're never so vulnerable than when we trust someone... but paradoxically,
if we cannot trust, neither can we find joy or love?
(unknown author)

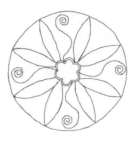

Day 4
Journal Prompt...

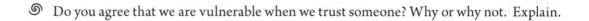

🌀 Do you agree that we are vulnerable when we trust someone? Why or why not. Explain.

🌀 What does being vulnerable mean to you? Are you able to be vulnerable with anyone? If not what holds you back?

🌀 Is there anyone or anything you trust completely? If yes, what makes it possible for you to trust? If not, what is stopping you from trusting?

*"We're never so vulnerable than when we trust someone… but paradoxically,
if we cannot trust, neither can we find joy or love?*
(unknown author)

Experiential Exercise

(Practice in trust)

Preparation for practice

Select a day for this practice. Give all your worries, anxieties, and concerns to God. You can imagine this by holding up your hands and letting it all go. I often imagine putting any concern into a white silk bag with a beautiful turquoise ribbon and throwing into a gently flowing river knowing it will make its' way to the source of all being and be loved and cared for. Find the visual that helps you let go.

Practice

On this day, you will practice not giving any advice or trying to control any situations or people in any way. Trust that all will unfold as it should without your intervention. When you feel you must intervene pray instead, saying I, trust all is as it should be and I let go of trying to control. Observe your thoughts, feelings, and emotions when you want to intervene but choose not to. Do not judge yourself or anyone else, simply observe without any desire to change or fix anything. This practice gives you the opportunity to understand yourself more fully. It is in understanding that we gain compassion for ourselves and the world around us.

"We're never so vulnerable than when we trust someone… but paradoxically, if we cannot trust, neither can we find joy or love?
(unknown author)

Holy Listening

(Read 3 times silently and/or out loud. Notice word or words that seem to be calling for your attention. Sit in silence listening to their message. Write a reflection.)

If you trust absolutely you will always be receptive enough to the signals that life and God and yourself-your deep self—will be giving you. You will always be given the clue, the information, and the inspiration to carry you through. *(Andrew Harvey)*

"May today you find peace within. May you trust in your highest power
that you are exactly where you are meant to be…"
(St. Teresa of Avila)

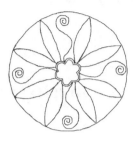

Day 5
Journal Prompts…

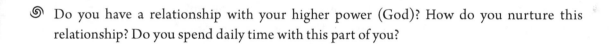

🌀 Do you have a relationship with your higher power (God)? How do you nurture this relationship? Do you spend daily time with this part of you?

🌀 What are the circumstances in your life trying to teach you? Are you taking time to listen to them with love and respect?

🌀 Describe as best you can your relationship with your higher power (God)? Is it like a friendship, parent, boss, teacher, guide, lover,… ?

*"May today you find peace within. May you trust in your highest power
that you are exactly where you are meant to be…"*
(St. Teresa of Avila)

Experiential Exercise

(Painting mediation)

The intention of this exercise is to help you express what is going on in your inner life without using words, which can often be very limiting. Using watercolors helps you notice the freedom in flowing in the moment. This exercise is completely about process and has nothing to do with the end product, so let go of worrying about what the result will be. Allow yourself to be present in the moment to learn what the paint has to teach you.

Select three favorite colors. Draw a large circle on a blank piece of paper. Sit in silence for a few minutes breathing slowly and deeply to center yourself in the moment. Let go of all concerns, worries, or things to do. Be fully present.

Get your brushes, water, paint and paper set up and ready to go. You can put on some favorite music to help you loosen up or you can just start painting within the circle. Do not think about what you are painting just become absorbed in the process. Watch the colors as you put them on the paper. Observe what happens when you add more water. Notice as the colors move together in the movement of the water. Notice how the colors affect you. As best you can, let your hand move as it wants without your mind directing it.

When you are done sit in silence looking at what you created. What do you think it is telling you about your inner world? How does it make you feel?

*"May today you find peace within. May you trust in your highest power
that you are exactly where you are meant to be…"*
(St. Teresa of Avila)

Holy Listening

(Read 3 times silently and/or out loud. Notice word or words that seem to be calling for your attention. Sit in silence listening to their message. Write a reflection.)

Serenity Prayer

God grant me the serenity
to accept the things I cannot change.
Courage to change the things I can
and the wisdom to know the difference.

Living one day at a time.
Enjoying one moment at a time.
Accepting hardship as the pathway to peace.

Taking as he did, this sinful world as it is,
not as I would have it;
Trusting that He will make all things right
if I surrender to His Will;
That I may be reasonably happy in this life
And supremely happy with him forever in the next.

"Trust in the slow work of God. We are quite naturally impatient in everything to reach the end without delay."
(Pierre De Chardin)

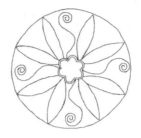

Day 6
Journal Prompts...

§ Is waiting difficult for you?

§ Think of an experience when you were forced to be patient. How did you react to the situation? What did you learn about yourself? What did you learn about waiting?

§ Why do you think patience is such an important practice of the spiritual journey? What is required to be patient? What gifts have you been given through the practice of patience?

"Trust in the slow work of God. We are quite naturally impatient in everything to reach the end without delay."
(Pierre De Chardin)

Experiential Exercise

(Practice patience)

Make an intention for a day to practice the gift of patience. Like anything, we have to practice something to get better at it. For this day welcome any opportunity that the circumstances give you to wait. Notice your first reaction when you are not able to accomplish what you set out to do in the time frame you decided. Try to welcome waiting as a chance to pray. Observe your inner conversation when things do not unfold as you planned or hoped for.

Practicing patience develops humility, which is the core requirement to grow on the spiritual path. As we wait, we are able to see how we get frustrated when life does not go our way. We are able to observe how we often live as though we were at the center of the universe rather than God. As we grow in patience and humility, we are able to see a situation very differently and recognize the importance of respecting and caring for everyone and everything around us. Patience gives us a wider lens of understanding and opens us to wisdom, peace and serenity.

"Trust in the slow work of God. We are quite naturally impatient in everything to reach the end without delay."
(Pierre De Chardin)

Holy Listening

(Read 3 times silently and/or out loud. Notice word or words that seem to be calling for your attention. Sit in silence listening to their message. Write a reflection.)

Do not look for a spiritual flower every day. Sow the seed, water it with prayer and right endeavor. When it sprouts, take care of the plant, pulling out the seeds of doubt, indecision, and indifference that may spring up around it. Some morning you will suddenly behold your long waited spiritual flower of Realization. *(Yogananda)*

"Trust in God with all your heart and soul. Lean not on your own understanding. In all your ways acknowledge Him and He will set your paths straight."

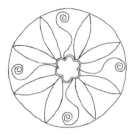

Review the Week
Day 7

🌀 Review your reflections for the week. Notice if there was a common theme that sticks out. Are there places where you would like to reflect more deeply?

🌀 What has this week's practices taught you about yourself? Have you gained any insight or understanding you did not have before?

🌀 Continue to notice each day where you trust and where you cling in fear.

🌀 Be grateful for the opportunity each day brings to gain in understanding, compassion and wisdom.

CHAPTER 2

OPENNESS

Introduction

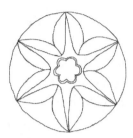

Have you ever thought about the sunflower as a messenger inviting us to open to the fullness of each unique moment? The long sturdy stem—rich brown center – and golden petals stretching to the Sun seem to ask us to root ourselves in our still, calm, center so we can stretch ourselves wide open and discover the petals of our true being. Could it be that the expansive openness of the sunflower is grounded in the rich brown center that trusts in the natural rhythm of life to supply all its needs in abundance? Is it possible that we too must learn to trust in the goodness of the universe so we can open our being into its natural openness and wonder.

This chapter invites you to be willing to let go of all that you think you know and open to the infinite possibilities that are born in the ground of trust. Allow the journal questions, experiential exercises and holy listening to assist you in letting go of the past, trusting in the future to help you open more fully to the gift of the present.

Personal Reflection

I know from my own experience that I spent much of my life clenched in a tight bud of fear that all the illusions of the world were true. That I needed to compete, compare, and earn my worth because there was not enough for all. I was told that I needed to be self-sufficient and only concerned about my own needs and the needs of those closest to me; that I was flawed and needed to be fixed because the creator of all was a being that punished. Indeed, I was taught fear was the ground of our being.

My inner world was suffocated in voices of self-abuse taunting me, blaming me into trying to be everyone but myself. I worked overtime trying to earn my worth; trying to be good enough and trying to please everyone around me at the expense of taking care of myself.

I followed the instructions very well; got married, had three children, lived in a beautiful house, sent the kids to private school, and went to church every Sunday. I had mastered the fine art of looking good on the outside while my inner world was a desolate landscape of anxiety running me in a million different directions looking to become filled, complete and whole.

The day came when my broken inner being shattered my outer masks into multiple sharp edged pieces of despair. I was plunged into darkness that only God could pull me out of. I was forced into surrender.

It was this experience of complete brokenness that opened me to my spiritual reality and set me on a course of true life in the divine creator, the holy one, the Lord of all.

Through this dark time, I was graced with new eyes that can see the light that directs me in each moment. I was given the heart of faith that knows I am being led to freedom, love and wholeness. I was given the wisdom to understand everything in the earth is a temporary stage set to teach me the spiritual lessons my soul came to learn. I was given the mind to understand that paradox is God's core language, which explains the reality that strength is experienced in weakness, light is discovered from the darkness, and hope is birthed in despair.

I learned that my true self is able to be patient, preserver and endure all things. I learned that simple small things bring profound joy. I experienced the wisdom of the sunflower; in my open vulnerability, I discovered the petals of my joy.

"When the pain of remaining closed is greater than the pain of opening the bud will blossom."
(author unknown)

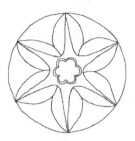

Day 1
Journal Prompts...

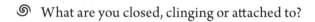

🌀 What are you closed, clinging or attached to?

🌀 What are you afraid to let go of? (Could be a relationship, idea, belief, concept, perception...)

🌀 If you knew all your material needs were provided for what would you be doing in your life?

"When the pain of remaining closed is greater than the
pain of opening the bud will blossom."
(author unknown)

Experiential Exercise

(Guided Imagery Meditation)

Before beginning the guided meditation, center yourself in your sacred place. Breath a few long slow breathes grateful for this time of inner reflection. Let go of all distractions and invite yourself to be fully present.

Imagine yourself in a dark forest late at night all alone. It is cold, dark and damp. You find a large tree to sit under and lean your back on the sure rooted trunk. You pull your knees to your chest and sit tightly huddled for protection.

Allow yourself to be fully present to being alone in this cold, dark, damp forest. Notice your body's reaction. Notice how your skin feels, how you are breathing, and what your mind is thinking. Are you afraid? What are you afraid of? (stay in this place in silence for a few minutes just observing yourself).

You find yourself asking for help. Speaking into the dark night sky, you notice a warm glowing light enfolding you, infusing you with calm, gentle energy. You notice the presence of this light enables you to unclench your arms and knees. You observe that your breathing slows down and your fear begins to dissolve.

A spiritual guide emerges from the light and sits across from you. Their open inviting serene presence opens you to many tears. Without any words, the guide invites you to share your fears, hopes, dreams, and challenges. Your heart opens and you share all the things that keep you closed and clinging. The guide listens as you empty yourself.

After a long time in silence, the guide asks you to imagine putting everything you have just shared into a raft and watch it flow down the river. Watch as the wind and the rivers current move them without any effort. Trust they will all be healed in God's time and grace.

*"When the pain of remaining closed is greater than the
pain of opening the bud will blossom."*
(author unknown)

Holy Listening

(Read 3 times silently and/or out loud. Notice word or words that seem to be calling for your attention. Sit in silence listening to their message. Write a reflection.)

Dear God

Open me
to the particles

Of Your Being

Fill me with
the music
of your
Love

Ripple me
in the spiral

Of Your Dance
(Margaret Coan)

"Confidence like art never comes from having all the answers it comes from being open to the questions."
(author unknown)

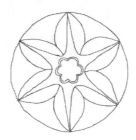

Day 2
Journal Prompts...

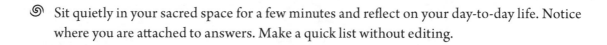

Sit quietly in your sacred space for a few minutes and reflect on your day-to-day life. Notice where you are attached to answers. Make a quick list without editing.

Is it possible these places where you have answers keep you closed and rigid in your thinking? Is it possible your answers separate you from the truth and your fellow man?

Is it possible that your closed-minded thinking blinds you to the infinite possibilities of happiness, love and joy?

*"Confidence like art never comes from having all the answers it
comes from being open to the questions."*
(author unknown)

Experiential Exercise

(Music mediation)

Sit quietly and choose a song that you love. Pray for the grace to have your heart softened and opened as you listen to this song. Allow any emotions the space they long for to flow through you. Be fully present to the experience and invite your imagination to bring you where the music leads.

After the music stops, stay still and imagine what you most long for. Where would you be? What would you be doing? Who would you be with? Include as much detail as possible in this imagining; colors, textures, sounds, smells, emotions, intuition etc… Let go of your practical mind and open to new ideas and new possibilities for your life. Remember, the truth, that with God all things are possible.

Write your longings, dreams and desires. What stops you from living them? What beliefs do you have that tell you your dreams are not possible? What fears keep you closed?

"Confidence like art never comes from having all the answers it comes from being open to the questions."
(Author unknown)

Holy Listening

(Read 3 times silently and/or out loud. Notice word or words that seem to be calling for your attention. Sit in silence listening to their message. Write a reflection.)

Have patience with everything unresolved in your heart and try to love the questions themselves as if they were locked rooms or books written in a very foreign language. Do not search for the answers, which could not be given to you now, because you would not be able to live them. And the point is, to live everything. Live the questions now. Perhaps then, someday far in the future, you will gradually, without even noticing it, live our way into the answer...

(Rainer Maria Rilke)

"Follow your bliss and the universe will open doors for you where there were only walls."
(Joseph Campbell)

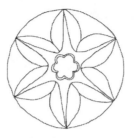

Day 3
Journal Prompts...

⑨ What do you love to do just for the joy of doing it with no care for the result or attention it may bring to you?

⑨ Use your imagination to create a day of bliss. Who would you be with (or maybe you would be alone)? What would you be doing? Where would you be?

⑨ What are the walls in your life? What stops you from opening the closed walls into doors?

"Follow your bliss and the universe will open doors for you where there were only walls."
(Joseph Campbell)

Experiential Exercise

(Free writing)

For five minutes, write without taking the pen off the page. Begin with writing:

I am open to _____ (fill in the blank).

After 5 minutes read your list and sit quietly.

Observe without judgment where you are open and where you are closed. Are there any closed windows in your life that you are ready to open trusting in the fresh breeze that will enter?

"Follow your bliss and the universe will open doors for you where there were only walls."
(Joseph Campbell)

Holy Listening

(Read 3 times silently and/or out loud. Notice word or words that seem to be calling for your attention. Sit in silence listening to their message. Write a reflection.)

When we don't open ourselves to the spiritual opportunities that exist for us, it is like living our lives within only one windowless room of a house, never having explored the rest of the house or gone outside to see what awaits us there. And within this one room, we focus only on our physical being – on our basic needs that keep us alive and fuel an egocentric way of being. When we share this room with like-minded people, we remain stuck within this physical place, unable to see the light of day that calls to us from the other side of the door. *(Judith Campbell)*

When we open the door of our heart to what beckons us inward, we become adventurers of the unknown territory of our being. We do not stay with what is identified and secure. We move outside the "one windowless room" and explore what lies beyond. *(Joyce Rupp)*

"Spend time in nature. Observe the natural rhythm for it teaches about all of life. Be open to the guidance."
(Author unknown)

Day 4
Journal Prompts...

What does nature teach about permanence and control?

What can we learn by observing the change of seasons?

What does nature show us about design, beauty, and symmetry?

*"Spend time in nature. Observe the natural rhythms for it teaches
about all of life. Be open to the guidance."*
(Author unknown)

Experiential Exercise

(Walk in nature)

Nature opens us to the wonder of our being. It is a place that opens us to all our senses and brings us a deep sense of connection to the mystery we call God. Notice what you see, what you hear, what you feel, and what you smell. How does this affect your sense of being?

While on your walk, try repeating a mantra. Choose a word that calls to your higher being. As you walk, repeat this mantra silently and allow your thoughts to flow freely as you rhythmically repeat your mantra. Notice how this practice affects your thinking and your sense of being.

*"Spend time in nature. Observe the natural rhythms for it teaches
about all of life. Be open to the guidance."*
(Author unknown)

Holy Listening

(Read 3 times silently and/or out loud. Notice word or words that seem to be calling for your attention. Sit in silence listening to their message. Write a reflection.)

Dandelion Puff

I long
to hold life
like a dandelion
puff

OPEN
to
each moment
as weightless
experience

FREE
To Be
the
Unique puff

OF MY BEING
(Margaret Coan)

"What we really want to do is what we are meant to do. When we do what we are meant to do doors open, money comes, we feel useful, and the work we do, feels like play to us."
(Julia Cameron)

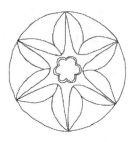

Day 5
Journal Prompt...

⚲ What are you living for? Are you living for your dream or someone else's?

⚲ What are you working for? (money, attention, recognition, or love , peace, joy, serenity)

⚲ What would you have to let go of to discover what you are meant to do or to live what you are meant to live?

"What we really want to do is what we are meant to do. When we do what we are meant to do doors open, money comes, we feel useful, and the work we do feels like play to us."
(Julia Cameron)

Experiential Exercise

(practice giving yourself what you love)

Choose a day where you will fill it with things you enjoy for themselves. You are to let go of all your should's and shouldn'ts and do only what you love. Practice giving yourself what you long for. If you are not sure what you love, try something new you have never done before that has interested you. Be willing to step into the unknown and discover a new part of yourself.

"What we really want to do is what we are meant to do. When we do what we are meant to do doors open, money comes, we feel useful, and the work we do feels like play to us."
(Julia Cameron)

Holy Listening

(Read 3 times silently and/or out loud. Notice word or words that seem to be calling for your attention. Sit in silence listening to their message. Write a reflection.)

May I, May you, May we

Allow our living to open us

To make us less afraid more accessible

To loosen our hearts...

(Dawna Markova)

"In oneself lies the whole world and if you know how to look and learn the door is there and the key is in your hand. Nobody can give you the key or the door to open except yourself."
(Jiddu Krishnamuti)

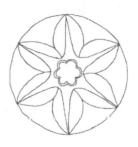

Day 6
Journal Prompts...

🌀 Are there areas in your life you are afraid to look at? Have you judged these areas as "bad" and do not want to look at the truth?

🌀 How do you think you find the door and the key?

🌀 Do you agree that nobody else can give you the key or the door to open? Why or why not?

"In oneself lies the whole world and if you know how to look and learn the door is there and the key is in your hand. Nobody can give you the key or the door to open except yourself."
(Jiddu Krishnamuti)

Experiential Exercise

(Practice observing without judgment)

This practice is one of self-awareness. Notice your inner responses and reactions to people, places and things. Notice your thoughts, feelings, sensations in your body, notice your judging thoughts. Do not label your reactions in anyway. Allow them to be as they are. Do not try to change them or analyze them, just be with them. If you stick with this practice, you will begin to notice that new awareness and understanding will flow from this space of non-judgment and acceptance for all your thoughts and reactions. It is important to not to try to change or fix, just simply observe without judgment.

"In oneself lies the whole world and if you know how to look and learn the door is there and the key is in your hand. Nobody can give you the key or the door to open except yourself."
(Jiddu Krishnamuti)

Holy Listening

(Read 3 times silently and/or out loud. Notice word or words that seem to be calling for your attention. Sit in silence listening to their message. Write a reflection.)

I am the one
who is grateful
for the
Wisdom of Experience

Who is opening
in a
rhythmic
Dance of living

Who bends
In the
Winds of presence

Stretching into
Limbs
Rooted in

Rich pungent divinity
(Margaret Coan)

Do not fear, trust in the joy of letting go and opening into beautiful blossom.

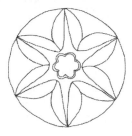

Review The Week
Day 7

🌀 Review your reflections for the week. Notice if there was a common theme that sticks out. Are there places where you would like to reflect more deeply?

🌀 What has this week's practices taught you about yourself? Were you open to seeing all the angels on your path and all the things to be grateful for?

🌀 Continue to notice each day the places where you are changing, growing and evolving into a more open and loving being.

🌀 Remember the spiritual life is a process of growing and evolving each day; be patient, kind and gentle to yourself as you practice each day.

🌀 Be grateful for the opportunity each day holds to open to new ways of living and understanding yourself and others.

CHAPTER 3

SILENCE

Introduction

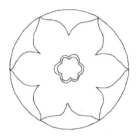

Have you ever thought about how a still body of water speaks to something deep within that connects you to calm soothing stillness? Have you noticed that still water is like a mirror reflecting all that is around it; creating an identical world in its reflection? Have you ever marveled at the infinite circular ripples that arise when you throw an object into the still body of water?

I have always been drawn to water for its language connects to something ancient within me. Being near water, heals, purifies, and calms my inner world. Indeed, water gently invites me to open to new landscapes within my eternal being.

Could it be that silence contains the same qualities of water that serve as food and nourishment to the soul? Is it possible, that like water, silence is a perfect mirror to our inner world as it reflects all that is within us? Have you ever considered silence as being the first and universal language that gives birth to all thoughts and words?

Just as an object that is thrown into still water creates infinite ripples, is it possible that our thoughts and words act as objects thrown into the landscape of silence that create and manifest our experience throughout the universe? Could it be that silence roots us to truth, wisdom, and knowledge and births creativity, love and being?

This chapter invites you to open to the divine language of silence and experience its sacred breath in your day-to-day living. As you practice the fine art of silence, ponder these questions in the reflection of your own experience. Silence longs to open you to your true being grounded in a still calm center.

Personal Reflection

As I reflect on my life, I am keenly aware of the constant noise that used to fill each moment. I moved in a rapid rhythm of endless anxiety as I tried to fill the inner litany of demands I imposed on myself. My body, mind and spirit were woven in a multitude of imbalance as I lived each day rushing around in endless circles of things to do, people to see, and places to go while my spirit was running on empty. I had created such a busy life and there was no time to live it.

I resisted silence because it opened my heart to feel the pain I had hidden in my closet of secrets for many years. I was swimming in the poisonous sea of shame, guilt and blame. The faster I tried to run from these parts of myself, the more they ran my life into a dark night of the soul.

Through this very painful experience, I learned the truth that silence is essential to the health of my being. I learned I had to face the parts of myself that I had abandoned in fear many years before. I learned that silence saves souls and God never abandons us even when we abandon ourselves. I learned that happiness and joy live in, with and through God and my spirit cannot live without the food of silence.

Learning to be still in silence feeds my body, mind and spirit at the roots of my being. I am able to see my inner world and love it in compassion. I experience silence as soaking in divinity the energy that heals all wounds and loves us into wholeness.

Silence has taught me the profound gift of feeling my pain and listening to its wisdom that creates wide-open space for abundant new life. Silence has emptied me of the loud anxiety that used to live within and opened me to the calm still being that lives in my center, your center, our center.

The practice of silence has transformed by busy, noisy life into calm serene stillness and I have ample time to be present and live each moment fully.

Silence beckons heed its call.

"Silence is God's first language, everything else is a poor translation. In order to hear that language, we must learn to be still and rest in God."
(Thomas Keating)

Day 1
Journal Prompts...

🌀 What has been your experience(s) with the practice of silence?

🌀 When you reflect on the word silence, what reaction/response do you have?

🌀 Write for 5-10 minutes without stopping starting each sentence of paragraph with silence
_____.

"Silence is God's first language, everything else is a poor translation. In order to hear that language, we must learn to be still and rest in God."
(Thomas Keating)

Experiential Exercise

(practicing being in silence)

The practice of sitting in silence is not to try and block out your thoughts, but rather give them space to flow in and out of your consciousness. The practice is to not attach to them or get engaged in their message. A good way to do this is to stay focused on your breathing. Pay attention to each in breath and each out breath. When you notice you are engaged in your thoughts simply bring your mind back to your breath with no judgment just attention.

Go to your sacred space and get comfortable. It is best to be sitting up so you do not fall asleep. If you fall asleep, that is ok but it is not the intention of the practice. The intention is to make room in your conscious mind for your unconscious thoughts, feelings, emotions to emerge for healing and release.

Be patient with yourself this is not an easy practice for most people; but I promise you it gets easier with time and eventually you crave it like you crave water. Just do one little step at a time and do not give up. Good practice in endurance.

Start this day with 5 to 10 minutes of silence.

"Silence is God's first language, everything else is a poor translation. In order to hear that language, we must learn to be still and rest in God."
(Thomas Keating)

Holy Listening

(Read 3 times silently and/or out loud. Notice word or words that seem to be calling for your attention. Sit in silence listening to their message. Write a reflection.)

Listening

I will listen
to the language
of my life
Accepting the syntax
of my present
experience
Not clinging to
what could have
been or
what will be
I will be
Still
Allowing Silence to
Break me Open
&
Empty
Me
Transforming the
language
of my experience
Into the Alphabet Of Grace
(Margaret Coan)

"There is no need to go to India or anywhere else to find peace. You will find that deep place of silence right in your room, your garden, or even your bathtub."
(Elizabeth Kubler-Ross)

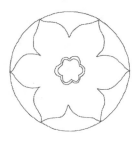

Day 2
Journal Prompts...

🌀 What places encourage and invite you to be silent?

🌀 Write a letter to silence sharing what you like about silence and what is challenging. Ask silence to help you become its friend.

🌀 What do you need to change to create more silence in your daily living? Observe what stops you from making new choices.

"There is no need to go to India or anywhere else to find peace. You will find that deep place of silence right in your room, your garden, or even your bathtub."
(Elizabeth Kubler-Ross)

Experiential Exercise

(Practice being in silence)

Throughout this week of practicing silence, you can always choose to sit in your sacred place in silence keeping in mind the intention of the practice as described in day 1 experiential exercise.

For this day, I offer another practice in silence. Try being silent at mealtime. Begin the meal by bringing your mind to gratitude for all the spiritual beings leading you on your path of transformation. As you sit in silence, become mindful of the food before you and give thanks for its love and nutrient to your body. If you notice, your mind is racing with thoughts of things to do, places to go etc. quiet it by a few slow deep breaths to become more fully present. The breath is a powerful practice that calms us and brings us into the present.

Observe yourself as you eat your meals in silence. Notice the gifts and challenges of the practice.

"There is no need to go to India or anywhere else to find peace. You will find that deep place of silence right in your room, your garden, or even your bathtub."
(Elizabeth Kubler-Ross)

Holy Listening

(Read 3 times silently and/or out loud. Notice word or words that seem to be calling for your attention. Sit in silence listening to their message. Write a reflection.)

Morning Invitation

Each Morning
I enter Into
Silent
Stillness

Legs Crossed
Back Straight
Heart Open

Grounded In
Simple
Space
I come
To Soak In
Divinity

Each breadth
A rhythmic tide
In... Out
In... Out
In... Out
Invites me
Into
Being
(Margaret Coan)

"The silence is within us. What we have to do is enter into it to become silent, to become the silence. The purpose of meditation and the challenge of meditation is to allow ourselves to become silent enough to allow this interior silence to emerge. Silence is the language of the spirit."
(John Mains)

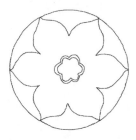

Day 3
Journal Prompts...

🌀 What needs to be emptied within you for there to be room for the silence to be opened?

🌀 What are you hiding within that keeps the door to your inner sanctuary of silence closed?

🌀 Write a letter to your fears that moves you away from silence.

"The silence is within us. What we have to do is enter into it to become silent, to become the silence. The purpose of meditation and the challenge of meditation is to allow ourselves to become silent enough to allow this interior silence to emerge.
Silence is the language of the spirit."
(John Mains)

Experiential Exercise

(Walking meditation)

You can continue to sit in your sacred space for a few minutes of silence or you can try a walking silent meditation.

Go to a beautiful place in nature to walk by yourself. Be silent and practice a breath mediation as you walk. On each in breath repeat in your mind "welcome silence…" and on each out breath repeat "I open to you…" When your mind travels to other thoughts simply notice and bring your mind back to the breath exercise welcoming silence. It may take awhile to get into a comfortable rhythm so be patient and persistent.

When your thoughts begin to wander gently bring them back to your Welcome Silence on the In Breath and I Open to You on the out breath. Give your thoughts freedom to go where they want and to be what they are.

You can write a reflection of this experience after your walk if you would like.

"The silence is within us. What we have to do is enter into it to become silent, to become the silence. The purpose of meditation and the challenge of meditation is to allow ourselves to become silent enough to allow this interior silence to emerge. Silence is the language of the spirit."
(John Mains)

Holy Listening

(Read 3 times silently and/or out loud. Notice word or words that seem to be calling for your attention. Sit in silence listening to their message. Write a reflection.)

Silence Weeps

Silence
Weeps
mist of stillness
upon my
soul

Opening its Breadth

On the
landscape
of my living

Speaking louder
than any
word

Silence
Deeply
Stills…
(Margaret Coan)

"Silence has many dimensions. It can be a regression and an escape, a loss of self, or it can be presence, awareness, unification, self-discovery. Negative silence blurs and confuses our identity, and we lapse into daydreams or diffuse anxieties. Positive silence pulls us together and makes us realize who we are, who we might be, and the distance between these two."
(Thomas Merton)

Day 4
Journal Prompts...

⑨ Think of a time(s) when you have gone into silence as an escape.

⑨ Try to remember the situation in as much detail as possible. Who were you with? What triggered the silence? How did you feel? Did this experience make you feel a loss of self? Did you feel more or less connected from the people you were with?

⑨ Think of an experience when you were silent and you felt present, unified, and aware. Did you gain insight about yourself?

⑨ When you sit in positive silence what do you observe yourself to be today? What do you believe you can become?

"Silence has many dimensions. It can be a regression and an escape, a loss of self, or it can be presence, awareness, unification, self-discovery. Negative silence blurs and confuses our identity, and we lapse into daydreams or diffuse anxieties. Positive silence pulls us together and makes us realize who we are, who we might be, and the distance between these two."
(Thomas Merton)

Experiential Exercise

(Practicing silence)

Today you have a choice to continue your silent time in your sacred place or try another exercise in practicing silence in your daily living.

Choose a day, or part of a day, to practice not speaking especially when you want to. When wanting to talk instead stay silent and observe your thoughts. Notice if it is difficult or easy. Notice why you want to talk. Notice how silence is a mirror for your inner thoughts. Remember it is very important to not judge your thoughts, simply observe. This practice helps you understand yourself more fully. It helps you become more aware of what triggers you, what you react to, as well as the places you are at peace and serene. The more we practice silence in all areas of our day to day life, the more we will open to our calms still center that awaits our

"Silence has many dimensions. It can be a regression and an escape, a loss of self, or it can be presence, awareness, unification, self-discovery. Negative silence blurs and confuses our identity, and we lapse into daydreams or diffuse anxieties. Positive silence pulls us together and makes us realize who we are, who we might be, and the distance between these two."
(Thomas Merton)

Holy Listening

(Read 3 times silently and/or out loud. Notice word or words that seem to be calling for your attention. Sit in silence listening to their message. Write a reflection.)

Silent Surrender

Opens into
a
sea of calm

A refuge
grounded
in
eternity

(Margaret Coan)

" Silence of the heart is necessary so you can hear God everywhere – in the closing of the door, in the person who needs you, in the birds that sing, in the flowers, in the animals."
(Mother Teresa)

Day 5
Journal Prompts...

🌀 What do you think Mother Teresa means by silence of the heart?

🌀 Could silence of the heart be when we are not reacting to the world, but instead, are able to be fully present to the moment in acceptance and gratitude?

🌀 Have you had an experience(s) of silence of the heart? Try to describe as best you can, knowing words are very limited.

"Silence of the heart is necessary so you can hear God everywhere – in the closing of the door, in the person who needs you, in the birds that sing, in the flowers, in the animals."
(Mother Teresa)

Experiential Exercise

(Practice being silent)

You can continue to sit in silence in your sacred space if that is nurturing your soul keep at it. If you prefer you can try the guided journey below.

Guided Journey

Enter your sacred space and sit still in relaxed position. Turn of all noise and shut out all distractions. Gently close your eyes and imagine a warm soft light warming every cell of your body. Allow this light to take on any shape it wants and stay focused on it. Watch it move from all your cells to your heart area. Become aware of your heart's response to the loving light. Be open and allow any feelings to be experienced and released. Breath slowly, steadily, and deeply. Let go of all that you know. Ask this light to bring silence to your heart.

"Silence of the heart is necessary so you can hear God everywhere – in the closing of the door, in the person who needs you, in the birds that sing, in the flowers, in the animals."
(Mother Teresa)

Holy Listening

(Read 3 times silently and/or out loud. Notice word or words that seem to be calling for your attention. Sit in silence listening to their message. Write a reflection)

Let Your God Love You

Be silent
Be still
Alone
Empty
Before your God
Say nothing
Ask nothing
Be silent
Be still
Let your God
Look upon you
That is all
God knows
And understands
God loves you with
An enormous love…
Wanting only to
Look upon you
With love
Quiet Still Be
Let your God
Love you…
(anonymous)

" Sit quietly, doing nothing, spring comes, and the grass grows of itself."
(Zen Saying)

Day 6
Journal Prompts...

🌀 Are you able to sit quietly doing nothing? If yes, describe. If not, what do you think stops you?

🌀 What parts of you need healing for the spring to come?

🌀 What are you not trusting to grow of itself?

" Sit quietly, doing nothing, spring comes, and the grass grows of itself."
(Zen Saying)

Experiential Exercise

(Practice of silence)

You can continue sitting in silence or try another practice using silence when you are reacting to a given situation. Instead of reacting in a given situation that often results in hurting yourself and others, try using silence as a sword that heals in awareness, understanding and compassion.

Next time you find yourself wanting to react to a situation, choose to go to a quiet place and sit in silence allowing yourself to experience your reaction fully. Listen to your body; is there tension that needs to be released; embrace all our feelings with love and compassion. Do not judge them or make them wrong. Feelings are not right or wrong they just are. When you allow them to be experienced they can be healed, released and new understanding is born.

" Sit quietly, doing nothing, spring comes, and the grass grows of itself."
(Zen Saying)

Holy Listening

(Read 3 times silently and/or out loud. Notice word or words that seem to be calling for your attention. Sit in silence listening to their message. Write a reflection.)

In the sweet territory of silence, we touch the mystery. It is the place of reflection and contemplation, and it is the place where we can connect with the deep knowing, to the deep wisdom way. *(Angeleo Arrien)*

"Holy Whisper, open the ears of my heart. May I hear your voice within the silence as well as within the noise of my life."
(Joyce Rupp)

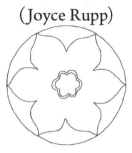

Week Review
Day 7

⟳ Review your reflections for the week. Notice if there was a common theme that sticks out. Are there places where you would like to reflect more deeply?

⟳ What have this week's practices taught you about yourself? Have you gained any insight or understanding you did not have before?

⟳ Continue to notice each day where being silent is a challenge and/or how silence is a wonderful refuge.

⟳ Be grateful for the opportunity each day gives to open to new ways of living and understanding yourself and others.

⟳ Reflect on how silence reflects your inner experience.

CHAPTER 4

FEELINGS

Introduction

Have you ever thought about your feelings as the language of the heart that inspires the musical notes of your experience? Could it be that these notes are designed to help us navigate the journey of our living? Is it possible our feelings our precious guides to healing, wellness and wholeness? Have you considered that every feeling has something important to teach us if we can learn to listen with a trusting and open heart?

Are there some feelings that you learned were "bad" and unwanted visitors and you mastered how to hide from them, cover them up, pretend they were not there? Is it possible in this process that you lost a vital part of your being that longs to be freed?

This chapter invites you to open to all your feelings. Allow the holy creator to soften your heart and heal all its hidden wounds. It is very important to stay connected to your higher self so that you will not get lost, stuck or abused in the process of opening your heart. Listen to your inner voice to direct you to all the support that will allow you to take this courageous journey. Trust that you will be led to all the angels waiting to walk with you and guide you through the darkness into the light.

Personal Reflection

My own experience of life has taught me that my feelings are sacred gifts of learning about myself, life, and all beings. I experience my feelings like notes in a musical composition that evoke a multitude of emotions and fuel movement in my day-to-day living. Depending on how I relate to my feelings (my perception of what they mean) they will either inspire, motivate, restore, heal, depress, suffocate, deplete or drain me. I have come to understand that my feelings dance to the rhythm of my limited perceptions.

For much of my life my feelings were running my life and I did not know it. I was blind to the power I gave them and to all the ways I hurt myself and those I loved the most in my lack of awareness. I was not able to see that I had lost my freedom of choice in my automatic reactions to people, places and things. I was imprisoned and blinded by my secrets and unhealed wounds.

Surrendering and opening to the truth and guidance of my higher power gave me new sight and understanding. I learned to observe my feelings and perceptions without judgment or desire to fix. God's grace asks me to open my heart to all my feelings, sit still with them, and listen to the wisdom they have come to share with me. Staying intimately connected to the Holy One enables me to empty out the dark shadows that I have spent life times hiding from and create new space for a wider lens of perception and understanding of myself and my fellow man.

As I have practiced observing without judgment or desire to fix, I have become aware of the reality of two primary sources that evoke my feelings; they come from fear or they come from love.

When I am afraid, I am prone to experience feelings of anger, resentment, bitterness, blame, shame and guilt. These feelings can rupture us, deplete us, break us, and even destroy us if we do not learn to listen to them, understand them, and embrace them in compassion.

When I am connected to the spirit of love, I am prone to experience feelings of peace, serenity, humility, compassion, understanding, and unity. These feelings can restore us, inspire us, forgive us, heal us, and transform us into our true divine nature.

I am profoundly grateful for every feeling I have experienced for they have shown me how to sing to the rhythm of my heart and dance to the music of my soul.

"What we don't let out traps us. We think no one else feels this way; I must be crazy so we don't say anything and we become enveloped by a deep loneliness, not knowing where our feelings come from or what to do with them. Why do I feel this way?"
(Sabrina Ward Harrison)

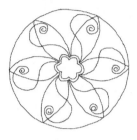

Day 1
Journal Invitation...

ⓢ What feelings do you have a hard time allowing yourself to feel? Sit quietly and allow the truth to emerge.

ⓢ Have you been taught these are bad to have? Do you judge them as wrong, bad; unkind... Is it possible your judgment is what stops you from being able to feel these feelings?

ⓢ Who are you hiding from? What might these repressed feelings have to teach you? Is it possible for you to think of these feelings as important teachers; guides to help you understand yourself more clearly?

"What we don't let out traps us. We think no one else feels this way; I must be crazy so we don't say anything and we become enveloped by a deep loneliness, not knowing where our feelings come from or what to do with them. Why do I feel this way?"
(Sabrina Ward Harrison)

Experiential Exercise

(Welcoming Prayer)

The Welcoming Prayer asks that we notice what's happening instead of reacting in one of our old ways, we instead welcome the feeling we'd like to escape. In that brief sliver of time between slight inner discomfort and the full-fledged reaction that pulls us into the same old hurtful places, we take a slow breath and welcome the feeling.

We let ourselves feel as deeply as possible the anger or suspicion or hurt, without pushing it away. We don't try to figure out what caused it, and we don't try to change it. We just feel it. We accept it as it is. And then we say "Welcome" and allow the feeling to surge through us, filling us inwardly. We don't project it outward onto others or keep it at bay; we still ourselves and let it pour in.

We give the feeling safe refuge, a place to belong. Maybe we even begin to hear what it's been trying to tell us all these years if we could only learn to listen. We open ourselves to receive whatever feelings come, *till little by little we find we can welcome all of who we are.*

"What we don't let out traps us. We think no one else feels this way; I must be crazy so we don't say anything and we become enveloped by a deep loneliness, not knowing where our feelings come from or what to do with them. Why do I feel this way?"
(Sabrina Ward Harrison)

Holy Listening

(Read slowly 3 times listening for word or words that seem to be calling for your attention. Sit in silence allowing the words to speak to you. Write a reflection)

This being human is a guesthouse.
Every morning a new arrival.

A joy, a depression, meanness,
some momentary awareness comes
as an unexpected visitor.

Welcome and attend them all:
Even if they're a crowd of sorrows,
who violently sweep your house
empty of its furniture, still,
treat each guest honorably.
He may be clearing you out
for some new delight.

The dark thought, the shame, the malice,
meet them at the door laughing,
and invite them in.

Be grateful for whoever comes,
because each has been sent
as a guide from beyond.
(Rumi)

"When she cried he would say 'there is nothing wrong with crying your feelings tell you who you are. They tell you what is important. Don't ever be ashamed of them."
(Terry Brooks)

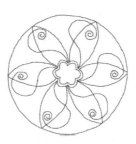

Day 2
Journal Prompts...

🌀 For 5 minutes write without stopping a list of feelings you experience. It is important to not stop, edit or think about the response.

🌀 From the list, which feelings are the most difficult for you to accept and experience?

🌀 What do you think these feelings are trying to tell you is important?

"When she cried he would say 'there is nothing wrong with crying your feelings tell you who you are. They tell you what is important. Don't ever be ashamed of them."
(Terry Brooks)

Experiential Exercise

(Body awareness)

Go to a sacred space that is quiet without any disturbances. Get in a comfortable position (can be sitting, lying down, standing, it doesn't matter as long as you are comfortable). Breathe in and out a few times very slowly and deeply. Use your mind to scan your body and just observe where it is tight, loose, sore etc. Do not try to fix or judge any of these sensations simply be aware of them. Nurture them in slow deep breathing inviting the energy to unwind. Be still and quiet simply being present and aware for about 10 minutes. After 10 minutes ask your body what it is attempting to communicate to you. Is it asking you to slow down, eat better, exercise, meditate, pray,… How is it inviting you to love yourself more fully? Is it communicating feelings that need to be felt and released?

"When she cried he would say 'there is nothing wrong with crying your feelings tell you who you are. They tell you what is important. Don't ever be ashamed of them."
(Terry Brooks)

Holy Listening

Your pain is the breaking of the shell
that encloses your understanding.
Even as the stone of the fruit must break,
that its heart may stand in the sun,
so must you know pain.
And could you keep your heart in wonder
at the daily miracles of your life, your pain
would not seem less wondrous than your joy;
And you would accept the seasons of your
heart, even as you have always accepted
the seasons that pass over your fields.
And you would watch with serenity
through the winters of your grief.

Much of your pain is self-chosen.
It is the bitter potion by which the
Physician within you heals your sick self.
Therefore trust the physician, and drink
his remedy in silence and tranquility:

For his hand, though heavy and hard, is
guided by the tender hand of the Unseen,
And the cup he brings, though it burn
your lips, has been fashioned of the clay
which the Potter has moistened with His
own sacred tears.

(Kahlil Gibran)

"Life is about trusting our feelings and taking chances, losing and finding happiness, appreciating the memories and learning from the past."

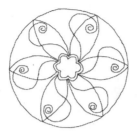

Day 3
Journal Prompts...

◎ Where in your life are you able to trust your feelings and take chances? Where is it difficult for you to trust and take chances?

◎ When in your experience have you lost and found happiness. Try to remember in as much detail as possible.

◎ What is your past teaching you today? Are there places in your life you would like to change?

"Life is about trusting our feelings and taking chances, losing and finding happiness, appreciating the memories and learning from the past."

Experiential Exercise

(Writing a memory in detail)

It has been shown that writing difficult memories in much detail including the sights, sounds, smells, people, time of day, weather, etc. is very healing. Think of a memory that continues to bring you pain. Sit still in quiet, breathing deeply and slowly to allow your soul to become fully present to this memory. Be patient as it opens to the experience. When it does start writing from your heart. Allow the feelings that may arise as you write to just flow out of you.

"Life is about trusting our feelings and taking chances, losing and finding happiness, appreciating the memories and learning from the past."

Holy Listening

(Read slowly 3 times noticing the word/s that seem to be calling for your attention. Sit in silence allowing them to speak to you. Write a reflection.)

One day you finally knew what you had to do,

and began, though the voices around you kept

shouting their bad advice... But little by little,

as you left their voices behind, the stars began to burn...

(Mary Oliver)

"When I step out on stage in front of thousands of people, I don't feel that I'm being brave. It can take much more courage to express true feelings to one person. In spite of the risks, the courage to be honest and intimate opens the way to self-discovery. It offers what we all want, the promise of love."
(Michael Jackson)

Day 4
Journal Prompts...

🌀 Is there anyone in your life you feel safe to express your true feelings with? What makes it possible for you to do that?

🌀 Who are you afraid to be honest with about your feelings? What stops you from being able to? Are you afraid of loosing their love or approval? If so, ask yourself the question is it really love if someone can not accept your feelings?

🌀 What stops you from having courage and taking risks in life? What are you afraid of?

"When I step out on stage in front of thousands of people, I don't feel that I'm being brave. It can take much more courage to express true feelings to one person. In spite of the risks, the courage to be honest and intimate opens the way to self-discovery. It offers what we all want, the promise of love."
(Michael Jackson)

Experiential Exercise

(Role-playing difficult conversation)

You can do this exercise either alone or with a friend you trust. Go to a private quiet place where no one will interrupt you or hear you. Set up two chairs facing each other. One chair is for you and the other is for the person you want to speak with about your feelings. You can put their picture in the chair or something that reminds you of them (clothing, object...). Before you begin speaking to them sit quietly and think about the things you really want to say, the things that you are unable to but you know you must to be honest and true to yourself .

Try to center yourself in your heart to access the feelings that are longing to be shared. When you are ready begin sharing what you, long to share. Allow yourself to feel the words; make space for whatever they are. After you have said all that you need to, you will trade places with the person you were speaking with. You will sit in their chair and imagine being them. You will respond to your communication allowing any feelings to be expressed.

At first, this exercise may seem crazy but give it a try it really opens up new understanding for yourself and the person you are having a difficult time communicating with. You may find the insights you gain from the exercise give you the courage to communicate what needs to be shared. You may find it helps you understand your feelings better and you no longer feel the need to tell the other person. You may find it was not possible for you to do. In any case, give it a try and see what happens.

"When I step out on stage in front of thousands of people, I don't feel that I'm being brave. It can take much more courage to express true feelings to one person. In spite of the risks, the courage to be honest and intimate opens the way to self-discovery. It offers what we all want, the promise of love."
(Michael Jackson)

Holy Listening

(Read slowly 3 times and notice what word/s are calling for your attention. Sit in silence and reflect on their message to you. Write a reflection.)

Honesty

Step 5 Al-Anon

Admitted to God, to ourselves, and to another human being the exact nature of our wrongs.

Talking openly and honestly to another person about ourselves, in an attitude that reflects self-responsibility, is critical to recovery.

It's important to admit what we have done wrong to others and to ourselves. Verbalize our beliefs and our behaviors. Get our resentments and fears out in the open.

That's how we release our pain. That's how we release old beliefs and feelings. That's how we are set free. The more clear and specific we can be with our Higher Power, ourselves, and another person, the more quickly we will experience that freedom.

Step Five is an important part of the recovery process. For those of us who have learned to keep secrets from ourselves and others, it is not just a step – it is a leap toward becoming healthy.

Today I will remember it's okay to talk about the issues that bother me. It is by sharing my issues that I will grow beyond them. I will also remember that it's okay to be selective about those in whom I confide. I can trust my instincts and choose someone who will not use my disclosures against me, and who will give me healthy feedback. Melody Beattie)

"Sometimes you have to forget what you feel and remember what you deserve."
(Author Unknown)

Day 5
Journal Prompts...

What do you think we each deserve in our relationships?

Are there people in your life that do not honor this? If so, who are they? How do they treat you? Why do you allow it? How do you treat them?

What would you need to change in yourself to have relationships where you get what you (and we all) deserve?

"Sometimes you have to forget what you feel and remember what you deserve."
(Author Unknown)

Experiential Exercises

(Imagine an ideal relationship)

Go for a walk alone in a beautiful place with the intention to ponder what an ideal relationship would be like. What would be required from each person? What would the relationship be grounded in? What would you deserve and what would the other person deserve? As you walk, ponder these questions keeping your heart and mind open to new ways thinking and understanding what a relationship is. Ponder who you have been in your relationships? Have you given to others what you think you deserve? Bring your journal with you so you can jot down any insights and/or understandings that may come to in the process.

The reason walking is helpful in the process is that walking opens us to our spiritual selves. Also, being in nature helps us connect to our own beautiful and true nature, which is able to see things outside of our own selfish interest.

"Sometimes you have to forget what you feel and remember what you deserve."
(Author Unknown)

Holy Listening

(Read, reflect, ponder how this speaks to your life)

Sacred Listening

Lord guide me
Teach me
Show me

How to listen with my heart

How to hear the questions
behind the answers

How to hear the hurt
behind the anger

How to hear the need
behind the accomplishment

How to hear the fear
behind the arrogance

How to hear the hope
behind the despair

How to hear Your Truth
behind every moment

How to always hear Your Love...
(Margaret Coan)

"Nobody can hurt me without my permission."
(Gandhi)

Day 6
Journal Prompts…

֍ Without taking time to think write without stopping for a few minutes all the people and situations that have hurt you in the past, hurt you now, and you are afraid will hurt you in the future?

֍ Reflect on the list while asking yourself the question, how has being hurt impacted my relationships with myself and other people?

֍ Reflect on your behavior when you feel hurt. Do you retaliate, hold resentments, become bitter or hopeless? Or are you able to allow yourself to feel the feelings in order to understand what you need to change to not be hurt?

"Nobody can hurt me without my permission."
(Gandhi)

Experiential Exercise

(awareness exercise)

Our feelings are important guides toward our inner healing if we can practice observing them without judgment and allowing ourselves to feel them without reacting from them. We react from feelings we are hiding from pretending we don't have them. In this denial, these feelings end up impacting our relationships in a hurtful way. By allowing ourselves to own all our feelings and not judge them as good or bad, we are able to become aware of them in truth. Through this practice, we are able to make a choice as to how we want to manage them. This exercise is simple but not easy.

Choose a day to become aware of your feelings by simply noticing them. It is very important to not have any agenda to change or fix them simply let them come to the surface of your consciousness. If you notice your mind judging them just observe that as well without trying to fix or change. If you start to feel some strong feelings, allow yourself to feel them by staying still and quiet. Remember slow deep breathing helps us open to all our feelings and give them space to be released.

"Nobody can hurt me without my permission."
(Gandhi)

Holy Listening

(Read, reflect, ponder how this speaks to your life)

There is nothing I can give you which you do not have, but there is much that while I cannot give it, you can take. No heaven can come to us unless our hearts find rest in today. Take heaven. No peace lies in the future, which is not hidden in this present instant. Take peace.

The gloom of this world is but a shadow behind it, yet within reach is joy. There is radiance and glory in the darkness could we but see, and to see we have only to look. I beseech you to look.

Life is so generous a giver, but we, judging its gifts by their covering, cast them away as ugly or heavy or hard. Remove the covering and you will find beneath it, a living splendor, woven of love, by wisdom, with power.

Welcome it, grasp it, and you touch the angel's hand that brings it to you. Everything we call a trial, a sorrow, or a duty, the angel's hand is there, the gift is there, and the wonder of an overshadowing presence. Our joys too, be not content with them as joys. They too conceal diviner gifts.

(Fra Giovanni, 1513)

Feelings are not right or wrong they just are.

Week Review
Day 7

🌀 Review your reflections for the week. Notice if there was a common theme that sticks out. Are there places where you would like to reflect more deeply?

🌀 What has this week's practices taught you about yourself? Have you gained any insight or understanding you did not have before?

🌀 Continue to notice each day where feeling is a challenge and/or how you are opening to your feelings and experiencing the release.

🌀 Be grateful for the opportunity each day to open to new ways of living and understanding yourself and others.

🌀 Reflect on how feelings guide and direct your life.

CHAPTER 5

HEALING

Introduction

Have you ever thought of healing like the rain? Sometimes it is torrential like a hurricane, sometimes strong like a thunderstorm and sometimes gentle like a summer drizzle. Have you ever noticed how the rain makes everything it touches radiant, pungent and rich in its cleansing lacquer highlighting the true essence in all it touches?

Could it be that we are healed in the storms of our living when we are ready to invite the tears to wash us into wholeness? Is it possible that when we decide to come out of hiding and learn to dance in our despair, we unlock the door to the kingdom of God waiting within? Is possible that our tears, like the rain, open us to our true divine essence of wondrous crystals of light?

Have you ever considered that the natural rhythm of healing is found in the language of surrender, forgiveness and letting go into acceptance? Is it possible that healing is as natural as breathing when we are connected to the divine source of unconditional love that is our true home?

This week invites you to open your heart to the rain that must fall. Listen deeply from your heart to the multitude of wounds you have been carrying for a long time. Allow the divine being to take these experiences and wash them in the balm of forgiving grace. Receive in humility and gratitude. Embrace the parts of yourself you have hidden to discover the wisdom they have come to teach you. Trust in the goodness of the Holy One; let go of your will and surrender into his so you can awaken to the true being of infinite love that you are.

Personal Reflection

I started hiding at a very young age as a way of protecting myself from all the critical voices that desired to form me in their own image. There seemed to be space for the "happy" me and no room for the "sad" me. I became a master of pretense learning to hide my darker side in the cave of my subconscious. I created many hiding places within my mind as well as within our house. I remember hiding every Christmas Eve so my Mom could find me and put me in her lap as we sang Christmas carols. I realize now that this game was my way of confirming that my mother loved me. Hiding became a life theme for me without me even knowing it. I became such an expert at hiding that I became totally disconnected from myself; I used other people's identities as places to hide. I became a stranger to myself; no longer knowing what my feelings were; not able to be present to what was because I automatically hid from it; too scared to allow it to speak and teach me.

My intimate relationship with Mary has graced me with the safety to dive into the hidden caves of my darkest shadows. Being grounded in the trust that she and Jesus will never abandon me I was able to dig in the darkness to find my true, trusting, loving, authentic self again.

I have learned that my dark sides have beautiful silver linings of self-love, acceptance, and compassion. Being graced with the courage to open my heart and allow all the hidden feelings space to be heard has healed my body, mind and soul. The greatest gift has been to find myself again. To be given the courage to burst my clenched bud and open to the wondrous blossom within.

I have learned in firsthand experience that honoring my feelings as guides toward wholeness and healing has enabled me to give them space to be released, loved and transformed and through this challenging process I am aware of heaven right here on earth.

"Healing may not be so much about getting better, as about letting go of everything that isn't you all of the expectations, all of the beliefs – and becoming who you are."
(Rachel Naomi Remen)

Day 1
Journal Prompts...

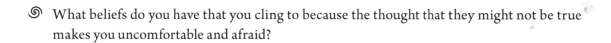

What beliefs do you have that you cling to because the thought that they might not be true makes you uncomfortable and afraid?

Is it possible that the ideas, beliefs you cling to most are keeping you from healing?

What beliefs/expectations have you been willing to let go of and open your heart and mind to a different way of thinking? What has been the result in your life?

"Healing may not be so much about getting better, as about letting go of everything that isn't you all of the expectations, all of the beliefs – and becoming who you are."
(Rachel Naomi Remen)

Experiential Exercises

(Burning Old Ideas/Beliefs)

Begin by going to a quiet sacred space and sit in silence breathing slowly and deeply to center your body, mind and spirit. Once you feel open and relaxed, ask your higher power to reveal to you the ideas/beliefs/expectations you are clinging to that are stopping you from becoming whole in the divine healing. Stay open and listen. Open your journal and for 5-to minutes write It would be healing for me to let go of _____ (fill in the blank). Try to do this exercise without thinking but instead writing from your heart.

After you have made this list read it over. Choose at least 3 things you are ready and willing to let go for your own healing. Write them on a piece of paper. Go outside and find a piece of earth where you can burn these pieces of paper in a ritual of letting go. As they burn say what you need to let them go; to know they are evaporating into smoke and leaving you with new space to observe and be present to the world in a more open and healing way. Embrace and accept any feelings that may express themselves in this ritual; thank them for their healing graces.

"Healing may not be so much about getting better, as about letting go of everything that isn't you all of the expectations, all of the beliefs – and becoming who you are."
(Rachel Naomi Remen)

Holy Listening

(Read, reflect, write how these words are speaking in your life)

Empty Into Healing

Empty me of
my wants
attachments
&
expectations…

Heal me in
Your love
Your grace
Your will

So I Can

Dance with the trees
Fly with the birds
Shine with the
SUN…
(Margaret Coan)

" We need to give each other the space to grow, to be ourselves, to exercise our diversity. We need to give each other space so that we may both give and receive such beautiful things as ideas, openness, dignity, joy, healing, and inclusion."
(Max de Pree)

Day 2
Journal Prompts...

🌀 What relationships in your life do you think need more space? Describe their current dynamics and ways that you might create more space for both of you.

🌀 What do you think is meant by space to grow? What kind of space do you need in your life to grow?

🌀 What would your life be like if you were true to yourself? Are there still areas where you are hiding from yourself and are not even sure who you are?

"We need to give each other the space to grow, to be ourselves, to exercise our diversity. We need to give each other space so that we may both give and receive such beautiful things as ideas, openness, dignity, joy, healing, and inclusion."
(Max de Pree)

Experiential Exercise

(Drawing/painting your space)

Select the media you would like to work with (colored pencil, markers, watercolor paints, acrylic, oils,) Choose a few favorite colors and paper, canvas or fabric to draw on. Before beginning, sit still for a few minutes breathing slowly and deeply thinking about your inner space. What does it look like, what does it feel like, what is it longing for? Try expressing these inner experiences with color, texture, design, shape. Remember it is the process of expression that heals not the end product. Try to be as fluid as possible letting your heart and hands to move in rhythm with each other. If you notice, you start thinking about what the end product is going to look like, let go into deep breathing.

If you are having a hard time flowing try putting on some favorite music to help, you open to your spirit.

When you feel you have expressed your inner space, sit still and observe your creation. What is it trying to communicate to you? Notice the shapes, colors, textures.

"We need to give each other the space to grow, to be ourselves, to exercise our diversity. We need to give each other space so that we may both give and receive such beautiful things as ideas, openness, dignity, joy, healing, and inclusion."
(Max de Pree)

Holy Listening

(Reflect, ponder, write how this is speaking to you)

"The only way beyond this experience
is through this experience.
Your only path to healing leads
directly through your hurting.
(James E. Miller)

"The practice of forgiveness is our most important contribution to the healing of the world."
(Marianne Williamson)

Day 3
Journal Prompts...

🌀 List the relationships in your life where you still feel hurt, wronged, bitter or resentful.

🌀 Who are you hurting by holding onto these negative emotions? Who would you be healing by letting them go?

🌀 Are you willing to ask for a humble and forgiving heart? Do you want to heal or be right?

*"The practice of forgiveness is our most important
contribution to the healing of the world."*
(Marianne Williamson)

Experiential Exercise

(Role-play with empty chair)

Go to your sacred place and set up two chairs facing each other. Decide on which person that you would like to start forgiving. Imagine that person sitting in one of the chairs (you may put something in the chair that reminds you of that person). Now sit in the other chair and sit silently for a few deep breaths. Ask God to open your heart and mind to what you need to say to this person so you can begin the process of forgiveness. Say everything that is on your heart, do not judge or edit what you need to say, simply say it. Get it all out; the hurt, the anger, the frustration,… Sit quietly and listen to what you have said.

Now change chairs; you become the person you are upset with and the empty chair is you. Now as the other person, you respond to what you said. Again, do not edit or judge simply respond from the heart. You may be surprised at what arises. When you are finished responding sit still and listen for the message this experience wants to give you.

Note: This may seem crazy at first, but give it a try it is very powerful.

*"The practice of forgiveness is our most important
contribution to the healing of the world."*
(Marianne Williamson)

Holy Listening

(Ponder, reflect, write how these words are speaking to you)

Ask not to be forgiven,
for this has already been accomplished.
Ask, rather to learn how to forgive.
Forgive the world,
and you will understand
that everything that God created
cannot have an end,
and nothing He did not create is real.
In this one sentence is our course explained.
What could you want
forgiveness cannot give?
Do you want peace? Forgiveness offers it.
Do you want happiness, a quiet mind,
a certainty of purpose,
and a sense of worth and beauty
that transcends the world?
Do you want care and safety,
and the warmth of sure protection always?
Do you want quietness that cannot be disturbed,
a deep, abiding comfort,
and a rest so perfect it can never be upset?
All this forgiveness offers you.
You who want peace
can find it only by complete forgiveness.
        . . . (Gifts From A Course In Miracles)

"Healing does not mean going back to the way things were before, but rather allowing what is now to move us closer to God."
(Ram Dass)

Day 4
Journal Prompts...

🌀 What is happening now in your life that inspires you to move closer to God?

🌀 What practices nourish your relationship with God?

🌀 When do you feel His presence most?

"Healing does not mean going back to the way things were before, but rather allowing what is now to move us closer to God."
(Ram Dass)

Experiential Exercise

(Time in Nature)

Go to your favorite outdoor place to walk or sit in nature. Breath slowly and deeply to become present to all the voices of God that abound in the natural world. Use all your senses to experience fully the now of where you are. What does is look like. What does it smell like? What does it feel like? What feelings are being evoked? Spend at least 20 minutes just being present to all that surrounds you with no agenda to say, think, or experience anything in particular. Allow the experience to unfold as it wants to. Be open to all that comes and welcome it with compassion and love.

"Healing does not mean going back to the way things were before, but rather allowing what is now to move us closer to God."
(Ram Dass)

Holy Listening

(Listen to, ponder, and reflect on how this is speaking in your life)

Bringer of truth, empty me of

whatever impedes the growth of our relationship.

Help me recognize and accept

Your sources for my growth.

(Joyce Rupp)

"The art of healing comes from nature, not from the physician. Therefore the physician must start from nature with an open mind."
(Phillipus Aureolus Paracelsus)

Day 5
Journal Prompts...

⑨ What do you think is meant by nature?

⑨ Could nature include all the truth that created and upholds our being?

⑨ Do you believe there is a natural way the body, mind and spirit know how to heal themselves? If not, explain. If yes, explain.

"The art of healing comes from nature, not from the physician. Therefore the physician must start from nature with an open mind."
(Phillipus Aureolus Paracelsus)

Experiential Exercise

(Body Meditation)

This exercise is grounded in the belief that our body has all the wisdom it needs to heal us; we just have to learn to listen. Go to your sacred place and sit still for a few minutes breathing slowly and deeply. Evoke the presence of the holy divine creator; soak in the presence. Now close your eyes and become aware of your body. Listen to each part from your feet to the top of your head. As you review your entire body notice any places where there are sensations that seem to be calling for your attention. Decide to focus on one area and visualize asking it in for tea/coffee. Sit across from this part of your body with the intention to listen to it and learn the wisdom it has come to teach you. Be still and quiet and then ask it "What are you trying to teach me? What am I not listening to? What can I do to love you more fully?" Stay still in silence and listen for its response; I promise you it will come. After you hear the wisdom then decide how you are going to practice it in your day-to-day living.

"The art of healing comes from nature, not from the physician. Therefore the physician must start from nature with an open mind."
(Phillipus Aureolus Paracelsus)

Holy Listening

(Read, ponder and reflect on how this is speaking in your life)

Be water
flow in non-resistance
strive not.

Hold all
lightly
as unreal
dissolves
Into
Real

Trust in
Suffering
as it
Washes Into
Whole.

Accept all
As it
Heals Us
Into

Home
(Margaret Coan)

"Love one another and help others to rise to the higher levels, simply by pouring out love. Love is infectious and the greatest healing energy."
(Sai Baba)

Day 6
Journal Prompts…

What do you perceive as loving? Name specific things.

What do you perceive as unloving? Again, name specific things.

Is it possible that your idea of love is limited by your own experiences? Could it be as you pray more and become more connected to your higher self you idea of love could shift?

"Love one another and help others to rise to the higher levels, simply by pouring out love. Love is infectious and the greatest healing energy."
(Sai Baba)

Experiential Exercise

(Breath mediation, walking meditation or silent meditation)
Today you have 3 choices to draw from.

🌀 Go to your sacred place and sit silently breathing slowly and deeply. For 15 to 20 minutes practice a breath prayer: On the in breath say I Am...

On the out breath... A Love Song

As you practice this your mind may have many thoughts, just notice without judgment and allow them to flow freely. Keep going back to the meditation.

🌀 Go out for a walk. Once you have a steady rhythm repeat the question love is... allow your mind to fill in the blank. Do not edit or change what appears; simply observe.

🌀 Go to your sacred place and sit in silence for 20 minutes using the word love as your sacred word. As your mind takes you on different directions simply repeat the word love very gently like a feather falling on snow.

"Love one another and help others to rise to the higher levels, simply by pouring out love. Love is infectious and the greatest healing energy."
(Sai Baba)

Holy Listening

(Read, ponder and reflect how this is speaking in your life)

Lessons I have learned about love through my grief journey – the process of letting go of attachments and expectations:

- Love lives in, with and through God our highest self.
- Love is what we are made of; our true home.
- Love holds no attachments or expectations.
- Love wants what is best for the other.
- Love does not try to possess, cling or demand.
- Love is patient, kind, does not envy, always trusts, and grounded in truth.
- Love thinks about purity, beauty and wholeness.
- Love is a daily moment-to-moment decision to be present to and to share in.
- Love endures all things, preservers, and hopes.

If I speak in the tongues of mortals and of angels, but do not have love, I am a noisy gong or a clanging symbol. And if I have prophetic powers, and understand all mysteries and all knowledge, and if I have all faith, so as to remove mountains, but do not have love, I am nothing. If I give away all my possessions, and if I hand over my body so that I may boast, but do not have love, I gain nothing.

Corinthians 13:

"We connect through listening. A loving silence often has more power to heal and to connect than the most well intentioned words."
(Rachel Naomi Remen)

Review of Week
Day 7

🌀 Review your reflections for the week. Notice if there was a common theme that sticks out. Are there places where you would like to reflect more deeply?

🌀 What has this week's practices taught you about yourself? Have you gained any insight or understanding you did not have before?

🌀 Notice each day where you are open to healing and allowing it to flow and/or where you are still clinging to unhealed wounds.

🌀 Remember the spiritual life is a process of growing and evolving each day; it is essential to be patient and kind to yourself as you grow and evolve.

🌀 Be grateful for the opportunity each day to open to new ways of living and understanding yourself and others.

🌀 Reflect on the necessity of surrender and acceptance as essential for healing to happen.

🌀 Remember all healing comes from love and the practice of forgiveness

CHAPTER 6

WISDOM

Introduction

Now that you have completed a pilgrimage of inner discovery I know you have stepped into many jewels of wisdom. I am certain that you have been invited to let go of many layers of lies and illusion grounded in the paradigm of fear. I pray you have grown in the faith of a loving Being who wants only what is best for you and all living beings.

This chapter is an opportunity for you to review the spiritual journey of the past five weeks; to cull the gems of wisdom created in your experience. Each day invites you to review each chapter again. Through this process of review you will become even more aware of your inner transformation and more open to expressing the pictures you long to paint, the songs you long to sing and the dances you long to dance.

Thank you for all the love and healing your journey is bringing to our world. As we open to our own healing we heal the world. Indeed, the greatest gift you give to another is a healed and peaceful heart that can hold the suffering in the sea of hope.

May the divine creator continue to lead you to your true home of unconditional love where peace and joy are the universal language of all being. May the healing power of forgiveness, surrender and acceptance guide you all the way home.

Enjoy The Dance For It Is Life.

Personal Reflection

Through my spiritual practice of moment to moment living, I have learned that wisdom is carved into our soul through our life experiences.

While knowledge is an intellectual understanding wisdom is born in the heart. It is not about answers but rather about learning to live in the questions and ride in the open spaces of the unknown trusting there is a loving being directing the course.

The language of wisdom is silence, humility and compassion. It enables me to see outside of my own desires to what is best for all. Wisdom has taught me that each season of life offers important life lessons. I experience my winters as beautiful as my springs, my sorrows as wondrous as my joys and my darkness as enlightening as my light. Paradox seems to be the core language of the divine, which I came to know in the sweet whisperings of wisdom.

"Wisdom is what is left after we've run out of personal opinions."
(Cullen Hightower)

Day 1
Review Week 1
Trust
Journal Prompts...

(Create your own or use the ones that spoke deeply to you in chapter 1)

"Wisdom is what is left after we've run out of personal opinions."
(Cullen Hightower)

Experiential Exercise

(Create your own or use the ones that spoke deeply to you in chapter 1)

"Wisdom is what is left after we've run out of personal opinions."
(Cullen Hightower)

Holy Listening

(Create your own or use the ones that spoke deeply to you in chapter 1)

*"One's first step in wisdom is to question everything – and
one's last is to come to terms with everything."*
(Georg Christoph Lichtenberg)

Day 2
Review Week 2
Open
Journal Prompts...

(Create your own or use the ones that spoke deeply to you in Chapter 2.)

*"One's first step in wisdom is to question everything – and
one's last is to come to terms with everything."*
(Georg Christoph Lichtenberg)

Experiential Exercise

(Create your own or use the ones that spoke deeply to you in Chapter 2.)

*"One's first step in wisdom is to question everything – and
one's last is to come to terms with everything."*
(Georg Christoph Lichtenberg)

Holy Listening

(Create your own or use the ones that spoke deeply to you in Chapter 2.)

"The art of being wise is the art of knowing what to overlook."
(William James)

Day 3
Review of Chapter 3
Silence
Journal Prompts...

(Create your own or use the ones that spoke deeply to you in Chapter 3.)

"The art of being wise is the art of knowing what to overlook."
(William James)

Experiential Exercise

(Create your own or use the ones that spoke deeply to you in Chapter 3.)

"The art of being wise is the art of knowing what to overlook."
(William James)

Holy Listening

(Create your own or use the ones that spoke deeply to you in Chapter 3.)

"The fool doth think he is wise, but the wise man knows himself to be a fool…"
(William Shakespeare)

Day 4
Review of Chapter 4
Feelings
Journal Prompts…

(Create your own or use the ones that spoke deeply to you in Chapter 4.)

"The fool doth think he is wise, but the wise man knows himself to be a fool…"
(William Shakespeare)

Experiential Exercise

(Create your own or use the ones that spoke deeply to you in Chapter 4.)

"The fool doth think he is wise, but the wise man knows himself to be a fool…"
(William Shakespeare)

Holy Listening

(Create your own or use the ones that spoke deeply to you in Chapter 4.)

*"Wisdom is the reward you get for a lifetime of listening
when you'd have preferred to talk."*
(Doug Larson)

Day 5
Review of Chapter 5
Healing
Journal Prompts...

(Create your own or use the ones that spoke deeply to you in Chapter 5.)

"Wisdom is the reward you get for a lifetime of listening
when you'd have preferred to talk."
(Doug Larson)

Experiential Exercise

(Create your own or use the ones that spoke deeply to you in Chapter 5.)

*"Wisdom is the reward you get for a lifetime of listening
when you'd have preferred to talk."*
(Doug Larson)

Holy Listening

(Create your own or use the ones that spoke deeply to you in Chapter 5.)

Wisdom is honoring my feelings without aiming them at someone else or letting them run my life.
(Hope for Today)

Day 6
Review of Chapter 6
Wisdom
Journal Prompts...

(Create your own or use ones that spoke deeply to you from chapter 6.)

Wisdom is honoring my feelings without aiming them at someone else or letting them run my life.
(Hope for Today)

Experiential Exercise

(Create your own or use one that spoke deeply to you from Chapter 6)

Wisdom is honoring my feelings without aiming them at someone else or letting them run my life.
(Hope for Today)

Holy Listening

(Choose your own scripture, poem, prayer, writing to reflect on)

Wisdom is becoming one with my higher power.

Review of Week
Day 7

🌀 Review the entire 6-week journey. What wisdom has been carved in the experience?

🌀 Are there sections you would like to revisit and pray with again? Remember each time we engage with something it is a different experience because we are changed each day.

🌀 What is next for you on your spiritual journey?

🌀 Have you come to know that you contain all the knowledge, truth, love and wisdom you need to find the kingdom that lives in, with, and through you?

🌀 Has this experience opened you to your authentic, beautiful, wondrous self?

As It Was In the Beginning,

Is Now,

And Ever Shall Be,

World Without End.

AMEN

About the Author

Margaret Coan's life experience as a wife, a mother of three sons, a caseworker for the homeless, and a bereavement counselor for hospice, has given birth to her gift of creating and facilitating sacred listening groups designed to support those in time of transition. Margaret and her family live in Maryland.

are going through a tough time because of the economy. All the wellness informati
in the last section made our life better emotionally! We felt better! Thank you!"

– Mark and Judy Гabec, Westlake, Ol

"I liked the information in the second part, "Soothing the Soul: Tips for Your Emotior
Well-being." I especially liked the thought about choosing to respond or react. I thi
it's important not to let your emotions guide the way you live. It IS a choice how v
handle situations with people. And let's be honest, people will upset you and thin
do happen in life. That idea was so helpful."

– B. Du.

"I fully endorse Nanci's wonderful book, *"Fresh Hope...Cleveland."* It was crafted by
woman who has found ways to make ends meet during tough times. Nanci has learne
what it means to "suffer well" by producing these materials to help others.

In my role as a pastor and clinical social worker, I am constantly reminded that peor
are searching desperately for hope and direction. Nanci has effectively addresse
both of these issues in her timely and practical book. The suggestions you will fi
on these pages are excellent reference points for people who want to pursue goc
wisdom, save money, and access vital local resources.

I believe her work is invaluable for pastors, counselors, church leadership, soc
workers — and most obviously, for people who are looking for concrete help. So mai
of us don't know what is available right in our own community. It is my desire that th
ideas and help she has compiled will find their way into many people's hands. Simp
stated, people need what she is offering.

I wish that more people would travel the narrow path like Nanci in seeking Go
serving others, and advancing Jesus's work in the world. She is clearly seeking
be both "heavenly minded" and "earthly good." I was encouraged and challenged
grow as a person and a Christian through reading her book. You will be, too!"

– Ryan Edlind, LISWS, Pastor of Care Ministries, Cuyahoga Valley Churc

Praise

think that often when people are the most needy, disillusioned, in pain, and
erwhelmed, this book would serve them exceedingly well. When I'm feeling like a
ser, sick, overwhelmed, or broken, or if "look-ups" aren't easy, I don't do them. This
ok would help anyone reach out and get support for what ails him or her.

iink in the many years that I have done psychotherapy, I have learned that many
ople could benefit from this great "what's the thing I should do now?" kind of book –
iich this certainly is. Easy to read and well organized; it will serve important functions
the lives of the unhappy, the needy, or those who want to find other good things
their lives. I know I'm into a set of great ideas when, as I am reading it, I want to
eate new stuff from that original idea, and I do with this book! It's an organized and
sy-to-use guide to doing things that will help people feel better right now."

– Walter Broadbent, Ph.D., psychologist

saved money because, as you suggested in the book, I didn't take my kids to the
ocery store with me. I figure I saved about $25.00 in just one trip to the store! With
em, they are always bringing other things to the cart which adds to my bill. Then,
course, I end up buying a lot of other things that I probably don't need. Too, I've
verted from the shopping list that was supposed to help me keep focused. That was
jreat tip or little recipe for my life!"

shopped at Goodwill after reading your book. I've never done that before! I found
and-new sandals for my son that still had the price tag on them! I got them for $3.00
nstead of $13.00. Isn't that great? Another great tip that helped me save money and
vould never have thought of going there before I read your book! Thank you!"

– Barbara Sponseller, North Ridgeville, Ohio

ie information in this book would be a good class to teach at churches. We really
ed the information about encouragement. You said in the book to write down all the

Printed in the United States
By Bookmasters